LANE VELVETEEN

THE BEAST CAME UNINVITED

THE AUTHOR

Lane Velveteen is the pseudonym of a sixteen year old who lives in Switzerland. She writes about topics that move her, mostly the interaction of so-called humans. Lane's language evokes strong imagery and emotions, at the same time beautiful and tortured.

Lane Velveteen

THE
BEAST
CAME
UNINVITED

Poems

All proceeds from selling the book go to the Halo Trust, a non-political and non-religious registered British charity and American non-profit organization which removes debris left behind by war, in particular land mines.

CONTENTS

CONTENTS

The Windy City Queen

I deeply, thoroughly envy
Liquorice gumdrop eyes looking at me
Razor sharp eyeliner on those eyes
Cheekbones as high as butterflies
I'm thoroughly jealous, so I become mean
Even though she's on the edge
The Windy City Queen

And she said

Why would you want to be like me
See all the things I'd wish unseen
God died a long time ago in my mind
I've got nothing to lose so I stay kind

And I

Set on fire all her advice
So I tried to fake it, fake being nice
Only, something went wrong, you see
Trying to be nice brings out the wrath in me

And I

Admire how she smiles through all
How I never see her fall
As she's trying to make small talk with me
Trying to see past all the jealousy
But all of this is just a play

Fake smiles to fake friends as if on a stage
All of her real friends just panic and...
"Are you okay?"

But I don't know what else to see
Other than a Windy City Queen and my envy

Don't

You, with your night sky hair
That falls down your back
What can I say
When the beast attacks?

You, who doesn't know
How to trust or love yet
The stars shine bright every day
Don't throw them away

I am the trinity of rose queens
And I say
"Don't tear me apart,
   Don't tear me apart,
      Don't tear me apart"

Made Of What, Exactly?

I am a rose queen
A beast
A violet
A demon
And the sun
All together, all at once
Seeing is believing
And peace will come
But how, no one knows
For it's not done
Shattered glass and cracking ice
I betrayed myself once
You betrayed me twice
I have two faces and two hearts
For every end I just restart

Your veins are filled with ink
Why do you never think
My veins are filled with lead
I'm not going to live until I'm dead
Plans are useless, plans are wrong
Nothing ever went as it should've all along
Nothing ever works out like the blueprint shows
Running after happiness only makes it leave, and go it does
It finds you when you chase after the abyss

Nothing beautiful asks for attention anymore
"Look at me! Look at me!"
What are you looking for?

Everybody's asking, but the truth now I'll say
"What is a personality?"
It's not like I want a real one anyway

You said you'd turn me into something
When the day was done
But if I keep on waiting, then tomorrow won't come

And then it was again, the trinity
Violets in my hair, sunlight on my face and me
I was looking for a place to shine,
But I searched and couldn't find mine
And then I knew that in looking for the dark I would find mine and
I did
Analyze, synthesize, conclude, begin
And don't put in any effort you don't want to put in

The lines have been filled
The parallels drawn
Awake, revive
The dark ends to reveal the dawn
And you are alive

The end is near
The beginning is near
And I climbed out the pool of tears
I am a beast, a demon too
And rose red, sunshine and violet blue

You Must

You went in first
All on your own
They sent you out alone
You said you wouldn't fail

But how can you stay idle in the face of this
You have to pick sides, and you have to exist
Do you want to leave or do you want to stay
Do you want to play the people, or want to get played
But it doesn't really matter
'Cause you just broke the game

All us wannabe golden girls, looking to the stars
West Coast
Walking down the boulevard
Roses in our hands
And moonlight in our hair
Thinking that we're different
But you see us everywhere

You're so west coast
That you are drowning
But you're something else
You're so quiet
Please just find yourself

What are you good for?
Why do you exist?
If you ever go, then you really won't be missed

Surprising

You have no soul
Was the verdict
I laughed and cried
As I heard it
I'm not surprised
Because while you preach peace and love
You didn't practice that, you slew the dove

You're full of fear, and you're already here
But you're barely alive
Constantly changing your identity is how you seem to survive

They call you a living scandal
Say you've had too much to handle
"now she's living through her fears"
How can you say you weren't in the city for years when you and
God know you were in the city for four years
But then again, how am I even surprised
You tell less truth than you tell lies

You say you should pledge allegiance and love one,
But you have come undone

Don't You Dare

Don't you dare to compare me with her
She's a killjoy. I'm a rebel.
She's scared of the world
And I'm the biggest extrovert you know
She went north-east
And I went south-west
You like her the least
But you love me the best
She's scared of attention
But it fuels my life
When we both have our guys
I'll be the better wife
Her life's a concept
But that would be the end of mine
She wears trash bags, but I'm a trend-setter
She's a wallflower, but I'm a go-getter

My Idols Are Cruel

Strangled by violets
Surrounded by violence
Sitting in the garden
You picked up the shards of the glass that shattered
You tried not to hurt yourself
But it's like walking on eggshells
You made yourself vulnerable
Next time, don't make yourself vulnerable
You know I hurt people
For I mocked an angel
And now everybody knows
Why did I not cry as its sweet soul died
Why do I want kindness if I repay it with ruthless cruelty
Why do you make yourself vulnerable to me

I tried to make an angel panic
I laughed as it became frantic
I prayed on my knees
As I giggled at its strangled pleas,
I tortured an angel, because it was everything
I ever wanted to be
And I took it with me, in all of my envy
I went to an angel's funeral uninvited,
And I stole a flower from its grave
As in death as in life it just gave and gave and gave
And I took and I mocked and I laughed in its face
I told all my friends I came here to make an angel feel envy
And then an angel appeared and then I just felt empty
I never stopped

Felt no remorse
And I'm still laughing here of course
I say that my idols are dead and my enemies are in power
But my idols are cruel, and I'm not in power
My idols are evil and fill me with envy
I take that rage and become everybody's enemy,
Make the whole world my enemy,
I tortured an angel, but an angel is still sweet to me

Into The Garden, Again

The sun's shining
In seven pairs of dark brown
Almond-shaped eyes
It's beautiful
The sun reflects off the grass
The trees, and the roses
It reflects in the joy of their souls
Soft rays play tag with the girl
And the boy silently stands in the glowing haze
The young man looks at the sunlit grass,
The young woman sleeps softly in its beams
The man is sitting in the sunlight,
And the woman is letting her soul warm up
The lady is softly crying due to joy and distress
[emptiness], [emptiness]
"Is that all of you", the sun seems to ask
Since it's been a long time

I. AM. READY. NOW

Not the pretty face that can do what's expected. Not
the perfect ace, and I'll leave you rejected, not the girl
that'll rise by the sea, not the child, or the edgy baby.
Not the girl you think you see, not the clone,
do you even know me.

I am somebody who never can produce a thing, because I spend
too much time trying too hard and worrying
they say one day you'll understand but nothing ever comes
Why should I spend time and live my life
When before I am even ready it's already done.

Am I as ready as I'll ever be
the adaptable ace that's how they know me
I sold my soul at the altar, I'm so long gone
But don't you think I'm ready now, please don't move on.

Ready set go, running off from the coast
You love me, you crave me, you want me the most
With all of their aggression, they venerate me
But I promise I'm not the girl they see

Now I understand what you wanted
You thought of me as cute, the youngest,
But I left you haunted
You only thought of me as my age
But then I asked for one more day

Sending out the signal, testing, testing,

Nothing's picking up, cause you'd rather be resting
Knowing that more we're all the same
The only thing we have in common is our name
You thought that you could understand
You caught a star with both your hands

With your long, dark hair and angel voice
You thought you wouldn't get hurt
But you made a choice
Now tears are flowing from your eyes
Your head is spinning why, why, why
You caught it and it ruined your life

The Verdict

Who am I to blame
You split apart
You ruined the game
The verdict's out
You're heartless
And these are all your faults
How were you all so careless
And so reckless
Just enough to fall

What happened to me
I said that'd you'd been good
I proclaimed my innocence
Out went my sense
And I did it all
I did it all
In the hopes that you would rise
And never fall
And now I realize

It's easier to put it all on one person
Say that she's a traitor
Make the whole world hate her
Not to bother with the game
And to only hate the player
It's easy to point fingers
To make one take one for the team
But nobody is perfect
Traitors are all three

It's too easy to idolize
And call you all angels
Then I woke up and realized
You'd be better off as strangers
West coast, 21
What happened to your rising sun
I then looked back and went to put you to the test
And now I ask myself where, how were you the best
You're no rose queens anymore
You took your roses and threw them to the floor

Sweetie, sweetie,
What a luscious web
You killed the dream
With all the backstabbing ideas in your head

Darling, darling
What a sweet poison
You killed the dream with your fake identities
And need for affection

Baby, baby
You only killed it softly
You killed the dream
With your family connections
And your skin and bone obsessions

My loves, you tore yourselves apart
Remember when you stood for beauty, and collective art?

I Am

It's funny how they call me vain
I'm always scared, always the same
Secretly I want to be you
But I am

I'm your hair that's thick and long
I'm your high-pitched voice in song
I'm your fear of slipping up
I'm your shiny trophy cup
I'm your husband
I'm your wife
I'm all the jealousy in your life
I'm your idol
I'm your muse
I'm your picture on the front-page news
I'm your moving van gone north
I'm the girl that pushes you forth
I'm your personality
I'm your grace
I'm your pretty little face
I'm all of the jealousy they all show
I'm your anger when they all say no
I'm your body
I'm your heart
I'm the fear that makes you fall apart

They say sugar and spice
Is what makes one nice
But jealousy's the poison

That makes me function
What can I say when I don't like what I've done
Because I'll always be the only, number one

I know you're fearful
You're an embarrassment to yourself
You're too scared to go out
Without anyone else
'Cause I'm just like you
I am all of your soul
Now you're alone
Isn't it tough to face your worst fear on your own
Laughter

Two Hearts

I disappear only to reappear somewhere else
And I I haven't heard of a sense of self
And I'm hypocritical in everything I do
You see me switching sides, oh well
It's true

Small heart, tall heart
Which one is me
And which is you
Small heart, tall heart
Which one is false
And which is true

Two hearts
Two minds
Two loyalties
We think that you aren't real
But they call you royalty
Small heart, tall heart

My only motivation is what benefits me
Shame on you if you don't agree
I play the game, cruel as I can be
And who cares if you lose, for you already lost me

Yes I say what I want to, when I feel like it
For I'm not aware of being quiet
Haven't heard of self-control
I may have two hearts, but I don't have a soul

Queen of Hearts

They said you knew the reasons that roses would be fun
But they just stabbed and kicked you out
Now you're the former one

Ha ha ha
I'm laughing
It makes me want to shout
Be wary of your false friends
For they'll help you find your door out
But don't know I'm one of them
And don't you know it's true
You think so highly of yourself
And set yourself up to lose
For people always come and go
Like actors playing parts
But underneath the roses
You're not the queen of hearts

They say you aren't a sellout
But who am I to disagree
For the standard of selloutery
Will always just be me

Roses, Roses, Roses
Off with their heads
Don't you worry darling, we're just painting the roses red
Roses with your pretty petals
And thorns that pin you down
Roses, roses, roses have come
And now you've lost your crown

What should I even say?
You make your friends want to betray
It's not my fault that they all leave,
What else am I supposed to believe?

In a world of saints
And in a world of sinners
You are just a girl
The only one
That was never a winner
Another chance, another miss
You realized you don't want to do this
Your head is filled with things unsaid
Wishing for the bloom of more roses, red

For Your Heart

The beauty who cut her hair
And the beast who has her back
And stabs it simultaneously
The beauty with once-flowing hair
Who used to be the target of all my envy
The beast who turned up uninvited
And the beauty who defended him
And the beast who can't stand her
And the beauty that praised and commended him

You know the beauty's obsessed
With being number one
You know you thought a rose queen
Was worth less
Than the troubled beauty that won
You know that you chose a traitor
Stop explaining how much you hate her
They took away your agency
'Cause you can't make decisions based in reality
And they'll celebrate the beauty with two hearts
Whose soul has been torn into countless parts
Singing:

For your heart
We'd do anything
Just for one
Just to celebrate
The decade
The anniversary

Of your treachery
For your heart
We'd even start lying
And slowly dying inside
For your heart
We've already died

Here's to a year
The year of the traitor
Beauty, liar, queen of hearts
For each of them a festival
And for the worst one,
"We've got to celebrate her"

The beast came uninvited on a nice, warm summer's day
And if you tell it to eff off it will not go away

A girl who got rejected
And didn't pass the test
Now not only represents the beast
But beat out all the rest

Happy anniversary
You have no more agency
You have chosen a traitor queen
Oh, the worst I've ever seen

X.V.

I once climbed into a shattered looking glass
To find that it was a shattered glass city
Is that what they meant
When they talked about a land of gods and monsters
Was I a god
Was I a monster
Or was I both
A poet who uses her words to paint, speak and emote
And a tomboy who gave up on using her words
Both afraid that no one would understand them
A diligent worker who did everything in her power
And a ball of rage and ambition that didn't
I wondered what the shards were
I found out, eventually
Why glass cities don't exist
And why once upon a time, one did
And what became of it
It was a wicked awakening
Having the glass city's shards being thrown into my face
But then again
I knew
You had lived with them inside you your whole life
My glass-ridden face, my glassy eyes, my glass-touched soul
Was nothing

Your shattered glass skin, your almond eyes,
Your shattered glass heart and your shattered glass city
Were the things legends were made of

A beautiful tragedy

Twice As Fast

I can build a city of glass
And I could tear it down twice as fast
What for, though?
My dear, what do I say to you
Yes I know, and yes, it's true
I'm not going against you, you know
If it would be sabotage, I'd have told you so
It's just....
I can build a city of glass
And while I couldn't tear it up at all
Some would gladly make it fall
And do much worse as well
And some would fix the shards we see
Put it back together, piece by piece
For anyone, even if they tore it apart
And even though they don't care for that, they love, and are good at heart
And one day, when things will be better
When you will pack your things together
And go to the garden, almost as if back to the garden
You'll see a shining city
Made of glass
All will go well, and you won't ask
Why there's no more shimmering shards on the ground
Because, you know
A shattered glass city is dangerous
You would walk on eggshells
Trying not to get hurt

And there are so many better things than feeling hurt
Due to something you love
So, even though it seems hard,
In those who are trying, have trust
And, truth is, if I could
I'd build you a city of glass
But sadly, not as good
But, nevertheless, I hope you understand

Okay?

When the beast has got your soul
When you feel the void and don't feel whole
Just remember, I'm here with you
You're here because the void in your soul wants to be filled
Because you weren't weak or fake,
So you became strong-willed
Just remember, I'm here for you

I didn't know that such a small rose
Could contain so much rage
Take a deep breath, put the beast back into its cage
You have me to vent to, go ahead
Release the beast's claws that are stuck in your head
Get some cold water, please take a sip
And think of nice feelings, yes, that's it

You are valid
You are enough
You are loved
You are tough

Breathe in, breathe out, do it again
And don't put in any effort you don't want to put in
Wrap a soft blanket around yourself
Everything will end up okay
Nobody is leaving
With you we will stay

Let's speak of nice things
Not the beast
Roses, city lights, or a warm place
Piece by piece
Self-care is important, okay?

First Impressions/Are Misleading

Oh hello there, little one
Come with me, come explore
Do you want to see even more
These are roses, and this is a queen
Her name is the Queen Of Hearts
And she's the worst I've ever seen

The queen of hearts,
She played her part
And this is what she said:
There's only room for one of us
And that means not for two
Honestly, don't lose your head,
Because, it's off with you

Once upon a time
Everything was coming up roses for the queen of hearts
Until a queen sent her back to the start
"Where is the new queen" we all scream and shout
"I am the queen of hearts, and I have thrown her out"

As you fell through the rabbit hole
Was it like you expected,
To bow before the queen of hearts
Only to be rejected
Just like the queen of hearts
By her false friends
From the start

You're so like me
That it's an art
We're two against the queen of hearts
Stronger together
That's what we say
For you're leading the path,
Oh, you're leading the way

The queen of hearts is evil
For everybody knows
Although she brought the whole world roses
She is a wilted rose

The queen of hearts is envious
For you have friends to call your own
And though she lives in Wonderland
You have a happy second home

i'm a wilted rose

Wow, oh how the times change
One day I was a rose queen
And the next second, roses are synonymous with scandal
One minute I have everything
And I'm burning like a candle
The next, I've already seen way too much to handle
Because how times change
Life is strange

First there was a golden queen
Oh, the best you've ever seen
Then finally, we were born
Then came roses with their thorns
Soon that left a wilted rose
Who knows where the future goes
Because I'm wilted rose

I love how you got rid of your self-hate
Only to find your daughters full of self-loathing
And I like how you think that you're revolting
Because who cares, and who knows
I'm not revolting anymore, I'm a wilted rose

And I don't know, if I lose hope
But if I do, please pray for me
For who knows where I will be

Hopefully I will find my way
And if all the roses wilt one day
And sweet as candy, tough as thorns
Who knows who will face new scorn
And see, oh, rose queen, your false friends
They have come and met their ends

Love To The City (omg, I was a mess)

I'm sending love to the city
Love that is pretty,
Love that makes you cry

Love that makes you numb inside for weeks
And makes you want to die

Now you're on a pedestal like your namesake king
And your darling's at the worst,
But for you, it doesn't mean a thing

I'm sending love to the city
Not the nice type
But the type
That makes your heart break
Makes you shake
Nothing nice
Some advice:

I'm sending love to the one, which looks above the city
Maybe she'll teach you that love was meant to be pretty

Glass Bubbles

She lives in a bubble made of glass
Waiting for the time to pass
As she gets protected from her own emotions
She's the ice queen,
As cold as the snow in which she carries her roots
She's fiery, like the flames in the land of fire,
In which she carried them from
She's as joyful as a toddler,
That has just discovered a bag of sugar
And she's as emotional, and full of tears... as ME
Since what happened. The event. The tragedy.
Why she left.
She's been one of the kindest souls I've ever known,
Except I never knew her before it.
I only know the after
The ice queen
The ice queen, protected of any joy, which makes her cry
The ice queen, on the anniversary of what happened,
Who decided that there and then, she would make sure, That she
would be permanently reminded of it.
The ice queen, protected by a barrier of angry friends
Not angry at her, but at him
He who made the event happen.
The soulless shell of a person,
Seemingly more rage than anything else
He didn't dare touch her. He killed what were
The beautiful moments and hearts dearest to her.
That's all you need to know.

If I ever met him, I don't think I would hesitate to destroy him
Destroy him, not physically, but mentally, as he did to her
And while she waits, not crying tears of joy
Us, the barrier of angry friends
Dark brown hair and dark, almond-shaped eyes,
The same color as the darkest abyss of despair she fell into,
After it, the event, that the barrier of angry friends
Told me about, swearing me to secrecy.
The ice queen, way-too-nice queen,
Who has been through so much
Who no matter what,
Just smiles warmly as she waits to cry tears of impossible joy

Flowers

A pink mirror
With its rose-tinted glass
Which I climbed into
I fell into a garden
Where they told me I could stay
They said that their hearts were all hardened
And that this time
I had betrayed

Was I an angel
Was I a demon or a beast
Which was I the most
And which was I the least
Or was I something in between

Why were the flowers talking
And all the flowers marionettes
All the flowers always fighting
All the flowers sick of it
All the flowers shattering
All of them surrounding me
Which should I stay close to

"My allegiance is to a beast" I said
And once upon a time, one would've screamed "off with her head"
And I promise I'm not faking it
And oh, at least I'm making it

I don't want my bloody rose
Don't want it anymore
I just took it by the flower
And threw it on the floor

Eyes

You think you're so charming
With those two orbs of light
Glaring at the sky
As you wait for your fifteen seconds to go by
Not you your fame will ever live up to them
And we all know
So here's the story of how your eyes stole the show

Eyes to the skies
There's a queen on the rise
Eyes on the prize
Just a small sacrifice
All dressed in pretty
All dressed in pink
Eyes to the skies for you lose if you blink

So you played like a game
Looking for the fame
Just pretty little girl with a pretty, easy name
To replace the real one,
Just like the personality you once had

You made me change my perspective
But where have you been
For you have the eyes of a saint with a cardinal sin

Couldn't you just have stayed put without wanting to give in
Who cares about you for my self-esteem would win
What a day to be alive
For you're looking up to the skies
But where will you be once you make your goodbyes

Golden Girl

Maybe being thinner might make you a winner
But I won't get compared to you
Maybe being lost might make you sad, sad, sad
But just how lost are you
Maybe seeing skin and bone
Might get you on the idol throne
But it won't get you compared to me
Steal the show, save the best
for last, so relevant that you don't have a past,
with an eternal spotlight
whose light was always too damn vast,
but underneath the praise and the twirls,
are you really our golden girl?

I want to receive praise
like no one ever did. I want
it all to myself. I can't help
being a golden girl who'll just
end up stuck on the shelf.

For you will be fake, until
you shatter and break, because
we all need a healthy dose of
reality, not a spotlight to live
healthily, underneath the world
of diamonds and pearls, show
me where, where, where are
you, our golden girl.

Traitor

Look at her! She's a traitor, I even have
every reason to hate her. Look at her,
with her head in the gallows, but that's
what she got, for being so shallow,
because she didn't care. Maybe being a
turncoat isn't great, but life's not fair.

I feel no blame, and I feel no
shame, she lost herself, while playing
the game, I know she did it for
the fame, but they blame her, all
she did was betray, it's easy
in every way.

I look at her, and her loss and lack of identity.
Is losing it all what makes one free?
For what would you do, if I did it for the name of a traitor?
Would you still hate me as much as you hate her?
Must I give up my looks and my name for the game?

Look at her, she disgusts me. Where
are her values, where is her goal? Give
me the contract, but I'm not selling
my soul. She makes me envious, but
I'll never be her, because she ended up here
no matter what she preferred

Sway me, but I'll never become a traitor,
For what she did I'll always hate her
I'll never become her.

Regression

You are so regressive, everything you ever
thought was a step forward wasn't the
least bit progressive, remember when
you had a personality that you could
show us, and a hope that you
could know us and most of
all you had a plan, to move
on as fast as you can but I'd...

I'd call that regression, those steps
forward were retraced, I'd call
that so-called success and shove it
in your face, you never succeeded,
you always tried, with your rose-
tinted mirror and false pride... I'd
call that regression.

Oh, so your sister's a saint, and
they say you're a queen, that you've
the best and most amazing thing that
we've ever seen, and they say that you
could be whatever, you set your mind to
But going backwards is all you ever did.

It's funny because once I also
saw your success, but now I know that
you've regressed, you're becoming everything
that I never wanted to be, but I
am the girl with the competitive aggression,
you call that the future, I'd call that regression.

Put it in?

No one wants to put in
Any effort anymore
With your rose-tinted mirror
Don't you ever get bored?
You're always separating
And I don't want to be a hater
But if you act like a traitor
I don't know what to even say
When you all just leave that way
Because we should go back to the start
When you stood for beauty and collaborative art
When you didn't want to put in
So they tried to put you out
But you always kept on going
And that was what we were all about
Or the time you realized that you finally were free
To sing and to connive
Only to be beaten by a girl who would betray you
When the next year would arrive
She lied to you
A hypocrite
She was so fake
Not even a plastic doll could top it
Not even you could stop it
Not even we could drop it
So you betrayed yourselves

you can't have both

you can't have both
the queen of hearts
she thought she knew it from the start
as she set out to be the worst, but also to come in first

the queen of hearts had no regrets until she saw the red paint fall
just to reveal the red roses underneath it all

The queen of hearts didn't want to fall, but she went through the
rabbit hole, and the queen of hearts though she could have the
opposites of none and all.

The queen of hearts she had no hearts, so she met a girl with two,
one of which was false, and one of which was true. The queen
of hearts led the roses to a flower bed, and just when she was
happy, the roses wanted her dead.

Because you can't have both, you can't have all, we saw your
rise, we saw your fall, we saw the rise of your false friends, you bet
that we will see their ends. Because oh, you're a saint but you
think you're a queen, you're the best and worst I've ever seen.
But where is wonderland when you need a helping hand?

The queen of hearts she was sweet and tart, and so we all found
out, and she and the two hearted girl found three girls that they
all put out, a golden girl who lived for the fame, and a girl with
nice eyes who got played like the game and a girl without a
sense of shame.

The queen of hearts, she went north west, after she left friends south east, to do something no one wanted, and reached out to the fearsome beast, her friends afraid, that she had changed, abandoned her, left her estranged, and no one even speaks a word about the king of hearts, for he was cursed right from the start.

The queen of hearts she played her part, and even through her pride, she wanted it all, she wanted both, and so her life she tried, but life has never worked that way, so all her tears she cried, because oh, she's a saint, but she thinks she's a queen, the best and worst we've ever seen, and all her life she wanted both, but of one you've gotta make the most. Because where is wonderland when you need a helping hand?

Made By

The girl that keeps looking up
The golden girl, the wannabe
The sister of a saint
The traitor, don't you hate her
The queen of hearts
The two-hearted one, with all her jealousy
Who you call royalty
The nightingale who died young
The girl who went in number one.

Aren't these the characters that made me
I'm made by the very characters that break me
Created in my mind to be a fake me
Because as I did they make me
Oh, miserable characters love company
For they are sick and cruel-minded
It's what they see in me, so they take to me.

Made of the very characters
I am
Two hearts, no soul, they're in control
I don't even need to pretend to change me
They take to me, become my personality
My character, my idols, and my idols, they are cruel
It's what they see in me, I see it in them too.

Starlight

Oh starlight, you say this game's your life
I gave mine up to play
You know it's not like my life was ever going to be the same
You say this is your life
I gave my real life up
Just to make it mine
Oh starlight, I gave my heart to play
Now I'm barely alive
I'm a little bit angry,
But what can I say
I'm dead inside, anyway

All the Same

But you're all the same,
You'd do anything for the game,
None of you have a sense of shame
None of you are best,
None of you are worst,
All of you are all alone,
Fighting for that throne,
And hope's not a reasonable sacrifice,
When you've used her for the throne twice

They All Missed

And you were once a girl,
On the coast,
With only one face,
Until you let the beast swallow you,
Now you're a real disgrace,
You thought of yourself as higher,
You thought you could fight fire with fire,
But first you went against our queens and won,
And they missed like the shining moon missed the rising sun

Three

So I guess I left you twice, crying on the floor, when both old and new abandon you, you'll be weeping even more, what about your two friends; let's just talk about them, to see how it will end...

Look at that girl crashing to the ground, I think it must be really hard when you're lost and haven't been found, first born to rule, now all alone, and also when you're at your sisters' throats vying for the idol throne...

Look at that girl who walked away looking for the fame, she's going to get played, as she plays the game, and she doesn't care, oh what a shame...

Sorry?

When I saw you for the first time, I couldn't believe my eyes;
I had a chance and missed it, and then I missed it twice,
Then I saw my chance and eyed it with both eyes, 'cause you
should do it if it makes you want to fall yet bubble up inside
you saw me
and you called me brave
Just because I'm not afraid to trash my pretty little face
I spent all night laughing at what I thought about you
when you were something else
I used all the destructive things you did to feel better about myself
crying while I laughed tears down
became the queen of hearts
just to choke on candy till my teeth fell out
wishing you'd hold a rose in front of my face and tell me to stop
like you're used to doing
but that was before I knew you,
so why should you have told me a thing

Wired

Because we didn't want to be fake,
So we became strong-willed,
Our souls are cold
Our hearts well chilled,
Because we've been wired from the start,
Our heads a mess,
A work of art
And we've played every single part
For you

„You write teen poems about teens"

Those times just trashed my babies
That's why they're so messed up
I want to know what happened
But I'll never know enough

I want to know why you're like that
But I will never know
Because you'll never open up
Your soul, forever closed

My babies never had a childhood
They're bursting at the seams
They never grew up either though
The whole world thinks they're teens

The Glitter

I am the glitter on the musty, dusty floor
You only love me because I treat you like a god
And you're all I live for
I would've died for you any day
You wouldn't live for me anyway

Diamonds

They say
"Those times were chaos"
They say
"Those times were hell"
But what should they expect from you
It's all you've known yourself

„Where Are You"

Where are you
I miss it
I miss it when you lived
I miss you being so happy about me that
You started excitedly rushing your typing whenever I wrote to you
I miss you not having to try

I miss only getting four hours of sleep a day because you were all
I ever thought of, day and night

I miss crying my eyes out and feeling numb for you
I miss it, I really do

I miss feeling so numb that I literally went out
Like a broken lamp and telling myself
This was the happiest I've ever been in my life

Because I now know
I didn't tell myself that, it was true

Where are you?

Again

And I am waiting
For nothing
Crying on the floor
Lying to myself
You said I was your favorite
But you really are mine
I don't like to admit it
But that's why
I'll wait that long a time

Like You

The sky is bright like you,
And I am sad again
This is the beginning
But it also is the end
I know it will be over
The moment you respond
It severs and it ties back up
Our twisted, awful bond

Gold, Freshly Spun

I guess I took your words and spun gold
Leaving you in silence
I guess for a while I tried to defend those
Who caused the twisted violence
To your soul
But if you tell me your story
Then I'll spin gold
I guess that you used me
But I also used you softly
For it was more disturbing than anything
Anyone had ever put before me

When I Cry

I spin gold
But do one thing best
When I cry, I'm prettiest
I'm velvet soft
With thorns that sting
Oh, can't you see
I'm revolting
Air-like
I keep you alive
Steadily, steadily
I'm sweet
But just as deadly
Oh, I think I'm winning
Because you see,
You can fight back
But you'll always need me
But there's one thing you don't know
And that's that I need you
But if I tell
Then I'll seem weak
And if I do
It'll be the end of me

Pulled In

With you, it's all I ever wanted
This is my world
With my envy and adoration
Here is my world
With its characters and personalities
You'll be pulled in too
Into the hole
And just like me
You'll want to desperately get out and stay at the same time

GO PICK UP THE PIECES!!

She looks just like me
But she acts like a machine
For she is not a human
And she's never been

She's soulless
Heartless
An all around mess
Whose life is being slowly ripped to pieces

GO PICK UP THE PIECES!!

Bliss?

How could I stay idle in the face of this
If I don't think at all then I don't have to exist
Little One, Drama King and the Queen of Hearts
Honestly, they all are bad
All wilted rose has-beens
My little one, immoral now
I stare into the face of a dream
Life is strange
And now we all know
But sadly c'est la vie
La vie en wilted rose
And you my dear, my idol too
Is doing what I'd want to do
Your pretty face, face of the dream
It's bittersweet and true

Lullaby

I sing to you a lullaby
I'll write it just for you
Of a city warm, a sky of light
A place you know is true
Of coasts and boulevards, the sea
A lullaby for you, my dear
Of tales, of cities we call glass
One day, you'll call them "here"
Of a windy city near the shore
I hope that you will dream
A queen that was like none before
While I sing half-asleep, you beam
Of someone cheerful, always bright
You'll dream of soon, with love
Of someone who for you, stayed up all night
Who watches from above